YOU CAN SAY AN...

Phony Moral Guidance from the Mouth of President Trump

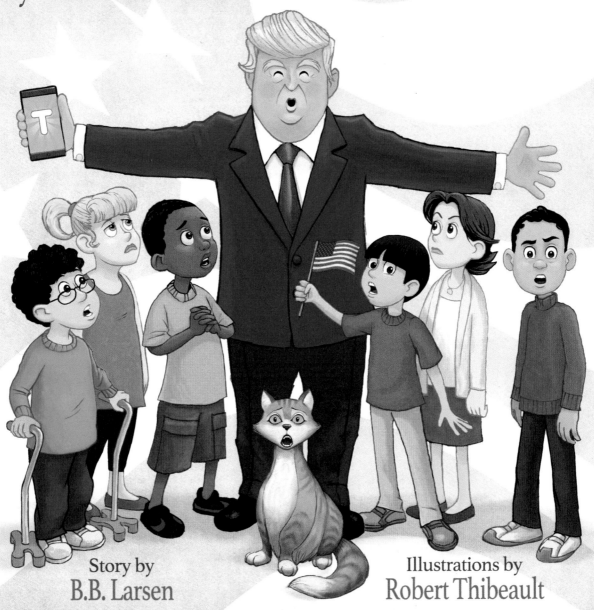

Story by
B.B. Larsen

Illustrations by
Robert Thibeault

PUBLIC NONSENSE PRESS

PUBLIC NONSENSE PRESS

PO Box 912
Norwood, MA 02062
www.PhonyMoralGuidance.com

Printed in the United States of America
First Printing, 2017
ISBN 978-0-6929-0942-3

*This book is dedicated to our future voters,
and in particular to Addie, Lily, and Lucas.
May they grow in a land that is less divided,
and more inspired by mutual understanding
and the common good.*

Come children, gather around, we'd like to share with you some of the words of our President, Donald J. Trump.

Before we teach you President Trump's lessons, we want to take you back to a time before you were born, when we think America was great.

So great, right? We're gonna make it great again.
Believe me.

Since those times, we know how worried your parents are about jobs being outsourced—*we tap right into your parents' fears!*

And, not to scare *you* too much, kids, but some refugees and other bad hombres out there might want to hurt you, and they could be really, really mean.

Everyone knows there are too many people in Washington with big money making decisions for you. We're going to clean that up; drain those big moneybags right out of government!*

* But first, we'll ease up on their regulation –too much bureaucracy!

And in the middle of all this, President Trump has some very helpful guidance for you...

...and you can say anything!

You can blame other people…

...define them in the worst terms.

Don't stop there. Keep calling your opponents names until the names stick like glue in everybody's mind.

Nothing is off limits...including appealing to our enemies for illegal favors.

"RUSSIA, IF YOU'RE LISTENING, I HOPE YOU'RE ABLE TO FIND THE 30,000 EMAILS THAT ARE MISSING. I THINK YOU WILL PROBABLY BE REWARDED MIGHTILY BY OUR PRESS."

Train your followers to depend on you for information, and to mistrust those PHONY fact–checking news organizations. SO SAD.

And, girls, we've got a lot of advice for you...

"A WOMAN WHO IS VERY FLAT-CHESTED IS VERY HARD TO BE A 10."

"IT REALLY DOESN'T MATTER WHAT THEY WRITE AS LONG AS YOU'VE GOT A YOUNG AND BEAUTIFUL PIECE OF A##."

"SHE'S OK. BUT SHE'S NOT A GREAT BEAUTY. I REALLY UNDERSTAND BEAUTY. AND I WILL TELL YOU, SHE'S NOT— I DO OWN MISS UNIVERSE. I DO OWN MISS USA."

Kids, you can really score laughs by ridiculing people who seem less fortunate than you.

It's easy to build support when you feed people's anger and fear…

... and lead people on with loud glowing promises.

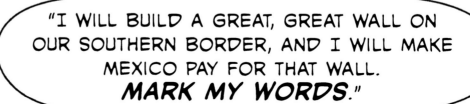

"I WILL BUILD A GREAT, GREAT WALL ON OUR SOUTHERN BORDER, AND I WILL MAKE MEXICO PAY FOR THAT WALL. **MARK MY WORDS**."

"FOR THOSE MINERS, GET READY BECAUSE YOU'RE GOING TO BE WORKING YOUR A##ES OFF!"

"I'M GOING TO BE THE GREATEST JOBS PRESIDENT GOD EVER CREATED."

You can even complain loudly about something that actually results from your own actions—and fire anyone who tries to determine the truth.

And kids—this is important! When you tell a lie, be sure to repeat it often and with confidence. Keep saying it until it becomes an *alternative fact*—some people will really buy into it!

You can always brag about whatever's on your mind…

Student Progress Report

Name: *Our Next Generation*

A	Cooperates with others
A	Open minded and fair
B$^+$	Works hard to complete tasks
B$^+$	Creative problem solver
A	Thinks of other's needs
A	Respects classmates
A	Listens to others

Comments: Our Next Generation is growing and learning. It is a pleasure to see your progress, despite the challenges thrown your way by previous students. We take great hope in your continued success.

Presidential Progress Report

Name: __Donald J. Trump__

- ☐ Cooperates with others
- ☐ Open minded and fair
- ☐ Works hard to complete tasks
- ☐ Creative problem solver
- ☐ Thinks of other's needs
- ☐ Respects classmates
- ☐ Listens to others

Comments: _____

_____

_____

_____

_____

Download form at: **www.phonymoralguidance.com**

Mail to: The Trump Household, 1600 Pennsylvania Ave NW, Washington DC 20500

Share the love (and the nonsense) with a friend!

Send a gift book or e-book:
www.phonymoralguidance.com/gift